D1526281

WE CAN READ about NATURE!™

WHERE ROBINS FLY

by ANITA HOLMES

BENCHMARK BOOKS

MARSHALL CAVENDISH
NEW YORK

With thanks to
Susan Jefferson, first grade teacher at Miamitown
Elementary, Ohio, for sharing her innovative teaching
techniques in the Fun with Phonics section.

Benchmark Books
Marshall Cavendish Corporation
99 White Plains Road
Tarrytown, New York 10591

Photo research by Candlepants, Inc.

Cover photo: *Photo Researchers, Inc.*, Steve Maslowski

The photographs in this book are used by permission and through the courtesy of:
Photo Researchers, Inc.: Kenneth W. Fink, 4; Rod Planck, 6, 12; Jeff Lepore, 7;
Maslowski, 8, 9, 11, 25; Anthony Mercieca, 13; James R. Fisher, 16; Adam Jones, 17;
John Mitchell, 21; Robert Carlyle Day, 22: Andrew L.Jones, 23 (top); Alan D. Carey, 26;
Calvin Larsen, 27; *Steven Holt*: 5. *Animals Animals*: Vicki J. Anderson, 10; David Boyle,
15; Michael Habicht, 23 (bottom); Bates Littlehales, 24; Patti Murray, 29.
VIREO/Academy of Natural Sciences: 19.

Library of Congress Cataloging-in-Publication Data

Holmes, Anita, date
Where robins fly / by Anita Holmes.
p. cm. — (We can read about nature!)
Includes index (p.32).
Summary: Describes the physical characteristics, behavior, habitat,
and life cycle of robins.
ISBN 0-7614-1109-7
1. Robins—Juvenile literature. [1. Robins.] I Title.
QL696.P288 H65 2001   598.8'42—dc21   99-057017

Printed in Italy

1 3 5 6 4 2

Look for these action words.

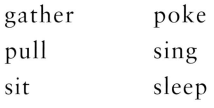

bathe	chirp
cock	crack
dip	drink
eat	feed
flutter	fly
gather	poke
pull	sing
sit	sleep
stop	stretch

Have you ever seen a robin?
I bet you have.
They like to visit people's yards.

The scientific name for a robin is Turdus migratorius.

Have you ever watched a robin
catch a worm?
It stops and cocks its head.
It looks and listens.

It pokes with its beak and
pulls the worm from the ground.

Now the robin needs a drink.
It dips its head.
It looks up and swallows.

Time for a bath!
It flutters its feathers in the water.

The robin flies to a branch.
It sings *cheer-up, cheer-i-ly, cheer-up.*

A group of robins is called a flock.

Then it flies away.
Have you ever wondered
where robins fly, and why?

Robins are busy birds.
In spring and summer
they raise their young.
Many fly north to do this.

13

First the mother and father gather grass and twigs.
They are building a nest.

Then the mother lays tiny blue eggs.

She sits on the eggs to keep
them warm.

Two weeks go by.

The eggs begin to crack.

18

Out come baby birds.
They are hungry.

These baby robins are one week old.

19

The babies stretch their necks.
Chirp, chirp, chirp!
The mother and father feed them
worms and caterpillars and bugs.

The babies grow.

Babies, or chicks, in a nest

A young robin, or fledgling, at about one and a half weeks . . .

. . . and at six weeks old

Soon they are ready to fly.
Their father teaches them to hunt.
Their mother stays behind.
She sits on new eggs in the nest.

23

Fall comes.

Days grow short.
Nights grow long and cool.
Some robins stay for the winter.

Many robins fly south.
It's warmer there.

Robins do not raise families in fall
and winter.
So they have lots of time—
to hunt and eat,

to drink and bathe,

to sing and fly about.

On winter nights
flocks of robins sleep together.
Robins chirp and sing before they
go to sleep.

Eeee, eeee.
Teeek, teeeek.
Tuk, tuk, tuk, tuk.

Good night, robins.
Sleep tight.

fun with phonics

How do we become fluent readers? We interpret, or decode, the written word. Knowledge of phonics—the rules and patterns for pronouncing letters—is essential. When we come upon a word we cannot figure out by any other strategy, we need to sound out that word.

Here are some very effective tools to help early readers along their way. Use the "add-on" technique to sound out unknown words. Simply add one sound at a time, always pronouncing previous sounds. For instance, to sound out the word **cat**, first say **c**, then **c-a**, then **c-a-t**, and finally the entire word **cat**. Reading "chunks" of letters is another important skill. These are patterns of two or more letters that make one sound.

Words from this book appear below. The markings are clues to help children master phonics rules and patterns. All consonant sounds are circled. Single vowels are either long ¯, short ˘, or silent /. Have fun with phonics, and a fluent reader will emerge.

Short "i" words:

d ĭ p s   d r ĭ n k   s ĭ p s

s ĭ t s   w ĭ t h   v ĭ s ĭ t

Bossy "or" says the word or.

n o r t h   s h o r t

Bossy "<u>ir</u>" says "rrr," as if an animal is growling.

ⓑ i r ⓓs   ⓕi r (s t)   c h ⓘr ⓟ
  rrr   rrr   rrr

If the "y" at the end of the word is the only vowel in the word, the "y" will make the long "i" sound. Long "i" says its name.

ⓑy ī   ⓕly ī   w h y ī

If there is a "y" at the end of the word and there is another vowel in the word, the "y" will make the long "e" sound. Long "e" says its name.

ⓑ ā ⓑy ē   ⓗ ŭ ⓝg r y ē   ⓣ ī ⓝy ē

fun facts

- The American robin is one of our country's favorite birds. It is the state bird of three states—Connecticut, Michigan, and Wisconsin.

- Baby robins are often fed more than three hundred times a day. While in the nest, a single brood may eat about thirty-two pounds of food.

- Robins sing loudest and sweetest at dawn and dusk. They are usually the first birds you hear in the morning and the last birds at night.

- Only the male robin sings.

31

glossary

chick   A newborn bird
fledgling   A young bird that has grown feathers
flock   A group of birds
Turdus Migratorius   The scientific name for a robin

index

about the author

Anita Holmes is both a writer and an editor with a long career in children's and educational publishing. She has a special interest in nature, gardening, and the environment and has written numerous articles and award-winning books for children on these subjects. Ms. Holmes lives in Norfolk, Connecticut.

ML   12/02